M′ ⸻ Y ⸻ RARY

⸻ ary,
⸻ el Street,
⸻ rick

FROM ⸻

ABOUT THIS BOOK

Downloading from the Net is an easy-to-follow guide explaining
how to download files essential to your computer's health, as
well as shareware for work, education, and entertainment.

THE ADVENT AND GROWTH OF THE
internet has made immense
amounts of data available for
downloading to the home PC. Finding
and downloading this data should be a
relatively simple operation involving little
more than clicking on a download button
and waiting until the file arrives on your
hard disk. But organizing how and when
to download files sensibly from the
internet can save you time, effort, and
money. With that in mind, this book will
help you to: organize and virus-check
your incoming files; decompress the file
formats commonly used by internet sites;
download entire web pages or only
selected text and images; find and
download maintenance files for keeping
your computer, peripherals, and software
running at peak efficiency; find the best
download sites; speed up your download
times; and navigate and use what are
known as FTP sites.

Downloading from the Net takes a step-
by-step approach to understanding the
processes described. Almost every step is
accompanied by an illustration showing
you how your own screen should look
when you follow the instructions.

The book contains several features to
help you understand both what is
happening and what you need to do.

Command keys, such as ENTER and
CTRL, are shown in these rectangles:
Enter⏎ and Ctrl, so there's no confusion,
for example, over whether you should
press that key or type the letters "ctrl."

Cross-references are shown in the text as
left- or right-hand page icons: ⟨ and ⟩.
The page number and the reference are
shown at the foot of the page.

There are also boxes explaining features
in detail, and tip boxes that provide you
with alternative methods. Finally, at the
back, you will find a glossary of common
terms and a comprehensive index.

ESSENTIAL DK COMPUTERS

INTERNET

DOWNLOADING FROM THE NET

BRIAN COOPER

A Dorling Kindersley Book

Dorling Kindersley
LONDON, NEW YORK, SYDNEY, DELHI,
PARIS, MUNICH, and JOHANNESBURG

Produced for Dorling Kindersley Limited by
Design Revolution, Queens Park Villa,
30 West Drive, Brighton, East Sussex BN2 2GE

EDITORIAL DIRECTOR Ian Whitelaw
SENIOR DESIGNER Andy Ashdown
PROJECT EDITOR John Watson
DESIGNER Paul Bowler

SENIOR EDITOR Mary Lindsay
SENIOR MANAGING ART EDITOR Nigel Duffield
DTP DESIGNER Jason Little
PRODUCTION CONTROLLER Michelle Thomas

Published in Great Britain in 2000 by
Dorling Kindersley Limited,
9 Henrietta Street, London WC2E 8PS

2 4 6 8 10 9 7 5 3 1

A CIP catalog record for this book is available from the British Library.

ISBN 0-7513-1300-9

Color reproduced by First Impressions, London
Printed in Italy by Graphicom

For our complete
catalog visit
www.dk.com

CONTENTS

DOWNLOADING BASICS

"Download it from the net" is such a common piece of advice now that it is difficult to recall when computers were stand-alone machines – connected only to the electricity supply.

WHAT'S AVAILABLE?

Most people are aware that the internet is an immense treasure-house of software and information, much of which can be accessed for free. Some of this material can be downloaded, which generally means transferring data from a remote computer to your own PC by means of a modem. So even browsing a web page involves downloading data files. To most people, however, downloading refers to copying a file from a site on the internet to their computer – usually to install and try out. Here are some of the most frequently downloaded types of files.

GAMES
These can range from simple retro delights, such as Space Invaders, to the latest commercial demos. Many games sites are devoted to software patches, fixes, cheat codes, screen shots, and software for games players to build their own playing levels in games .

**Specialist
Download Sites**

DOCUMENTS

The global library includes full electronic texts of thousands of out-of-copyright books, from Jane Austen to Emile Zola. Some text files are too large to be viewed as web pages and so are offered as downloadable documents to read offline.

www.tech-sol.net/interlinks/literature.htm

MUSIC

Playable music files are available in all audio formats including CD format, MP3, and WAV files. These extend from simple system alert sounds to complete albums. Sheet music, tablature, and other written musical forms can also be downloaded .

www.virtualsheetmusic.com/Home.html

IMAGES

Web-page authors will find many sites devoted to graphics (often available free for noncommercial use). Animation factory offers thousands of original graphics (including animated gif files) for downloading, as well as many other web-ready images and designs.

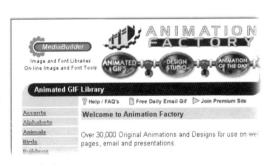

www.animfactory.com

SOFTWARE

If you visit any of the popular download sites featured in this book, it soon becomes clear that software accounts for most internet downloads. Programs are available for all types of computer, and in versions that will run on all types of operating system. The examples shown here represent only a few of the categories available to download and keep, or to try before you buy. These categories include document and image editing packages, and information and time-management programs, which can best be described as "productivity software."

WINFILES.COM
● Browsing through one of the many massive download sites is where a typical search for software usually begins. This example shows Winfiles.com.

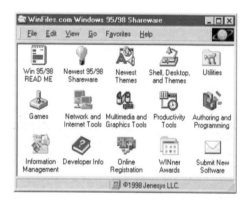

PIMS AND CALENDARS
● Personal Information Managers are available on all download sites; some are simply diaries and address books, others have features that will never let you forget a meeting, public holiday, or birthday ever again. This example shows Never Forget from Personal Reminder Software (**www.neverforget.com**).

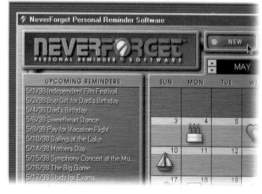

EDITING AND DTP SOFTWARE

● For the writer, there will never be a shortage of downloadable editing applications – whether you're looking for a simple freeware text editor, a freeware thesaurus/ dictionary, or a trial version of the most sophisticated desktop publishing program. This example shows the popular HotDog HTML editing program (**www.sausage.com**).

IMAGE EDITORS

● Sometimes it is preferable to use a simple, fast-loading image editor when you need to view a file quickly or convert it from one format to another. It is common for web editors to use several image editors during the same session. The Irfan image viewer (from **www.irfanview.com**) has been a consistently popular download over the last couple of years.

EQUIPMENT OPTIONS

If your PC is running Microsoft Windows 98, your computer is more than capable of efficiently downloading virtually all kinds of material from the internet. What will make the final difference to the time that you spend downloading each file is the type of modem you have and the type of connection that you are using.

THE 56K MODEM

The most popular modem is the 56K modem. The figure, 56K, refers to the speed at which the modem can receive data, i.e., at 56 kilobits per second. You can download files with a slower modem, but it obviously takes longer.

The modem shown above is the Hayes Accura 56K Speakerphone.

THE ISDN OPTION

An ISDN (*Integrated Services Digital Network)* connection, offers much higher data transfer speeds and two telephone lines, which allows you to access the internet and have a telephone conversation simultaneously. ISDN requires special hardware, software, a different telephone connection, and an ISP account.

COMPARATIVE MODEM SPEEDS	
MODEM TYPE	SPEED
Analog	
14.4K	14.4Kbps
28.8K	28.8kbps
56K	56Kbps
ISDN (Integrated Services Digital Network)	128Kbps
Cable	Up to 10 Mbps
Satellite	200-400Kbps
ADSL (Asynchronous Digital Subscriber Line)	512Kbps

EVEN FASTER OPTIONS

Other connection options can offer extraordinarily fast download speeds. These include cable modems – offering internet access via cable TV companies' lines; satellite modems – requiring a satellite dish with line of sight to the satellite; and digital subscriber line (DSL) technologies. The last option, (usually offered as ADSL where the letter A stands for Asynchronous), has the potential to deliver download speeds of millions of bits per second. An ADSL connection is permanently active and enables simultaneous web access and telephone use.

DOWNLOADING DIALOG BOX

● While you are downloading a file, a dialog box appears showing the estimated time remaining and the transfer rate, which can vary considerably during the download. Many download sites give helpful estimates of how long a download will take for particular modems.

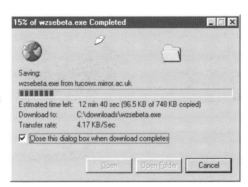

15% of wzsebeta.exe Completed

Saving:
wzsebeta.exe from tucows.mirror.ac.uk

Estimated time left: 12 min 40 sec (96.5 KB of 748 KB copied)
Download to: C:\downloads\wzsebeta.exe
Transfer rate: 4.17 KB/Sec

☑ Close this dialog box when download completes

Open | Open Folder | Cancel

DOWNLOAD SPEED RESTRICTIONS

Despite the claims of your ISP and the manufacturer of your modem, a 56k modem will hardly ever download information at 56k. The average rate is between 44k and 48k, but this can vary for a number of reasons.

For example:
● There may be overall congestion on the internet meaning that your ISP is receiving data at a slower rate than usual.
● Too many people are trying to access the site to which you are connecting.

● Your ISP has too few modems making the user-to-modem ratio too low.
● There is too much "noise" interfering with your telephone line.
● Your Windows 98 modem drivers may be old and need updating 🗋.

Downloading
31 **Device Drivers**

VARIATIONS IN CONNECTION SPEED

You can see the connection speed between you and your ISP by holding the mouse pointer over the modem icon on the taskbar while you have an active connection. These examples show variations when connecting to the same ISP during a five-minute period.

The first, slower, download speed •

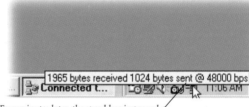

Four minutes later, the speed has improved •

DOWNLOAD PROBLEMS

Everyone will experience problems at some time when downloading files. The exact nature of the problem will usually be the result of one or more factors caused by hardware, software, your internet connection, your Internet Service Provider's software, or one of the connections between you, your ISP, and any of the other thousands of connections between you and the server from which you are trying to download the software. Considering the complexity of all these connections, it's amazing that any download is successful!

There are certain basic rules you can follow, however, when your connection drops. If you can't connect to the download site, or your connection is very slow, give up and try again later when there may be less communications traffic. If you are offered a choice of servers for the download, select one of the others – even if they are in a different country from your own.

If everything has locked, cancel the connection and try to connect again. Finally, you could try looking for software that offers enhanced downloading capabilities.

ORGANIZING YOUR HARD DRIVE

To avoid confusion as you download more and more files, you could set aside an area of your hard disk for incoming data. With a separate area, you won't have to spend time hunting for files you downloaded earlier that session; you reduce the chances of downloading the same file twice; and you can run your virus checker on a whole folder or the whole download folder after downloading several files.

DOWNLOAD FOLDER

● In the majority of cases when you download from the internet, you will have the opportunity to decide where the software will be placed on your hard drive. The best solution is to create a new folder on your hard drive and name it **downloads**.

● This example shows a few possible subfolders that could be included within a **downloads** folder on the C: drive. The subfolders that have been created are a typical range of software download categories.

Folder for software upgrades ●

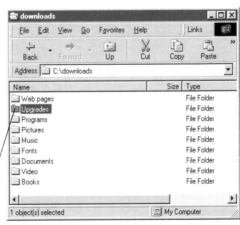

CHECK AND UNZIP

Before you begin downloading, you will need a virus checker to detect and destroy any viruses, and a decompression program to unlock compressed file formats.

ANTIVIRUS SOFTWARE

Every time you introduce a new file or install a new program on your computer via a floppy disk, CD, email, or the internet, you run the risk of introducing a virus onto your system. For this reason, a new computer may contain pre-installed virus-checking software that has been configured to scan the contents of your

hard disk at regular intervals and to scan incoming data, for example, when receiving an email or when inserting a floppy disk into the drive. In addition to this checking configuration, it is important that you run a virus scan on any program or file as soon as it has been downloaded to your computer.

OBTAINING A VIRUS CHECKER

If you do not have a virus checker, it is highly advisable that you obtain one as soon as possible, certainly before you begin downloading from the internet. Virus checkers are available from your software store, online from a manufacturer, or from software download sites. The following examples show how to download try-before-you-buy versions of two of the leading virus checkers available today.

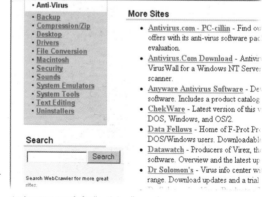

An internet search for "antivirus" reveals many downloadable antivirus programs.

DOWNLOADING A TRIAL VERSION

There are many antivirus programs available for downloading as freeware, shareware, or as trial versions of commercial software. Two of the most widely used products are McAfee.Com Clinic and Symantec's Norton AntiVirus, but there are many other well-regarded products available for downloading from many of the shareware sites referred to in this book 📄. Which virus detection software you use is a matter of individual choice based on advice and personal preference. You will usually be offered a trial period – typically 30 days – which will be long enough for you to choose the software that best suits your requirements.

MCAFEE.COM CLINIC

● You can find McAfee's main web page at **www. mcafee.com**. McAfee.com Clinic contains a virus checker as well as other computer maintenance and management software.

● Click the **Free Trial** button to begin the downloading process, during which you will need to complete a customer information form.

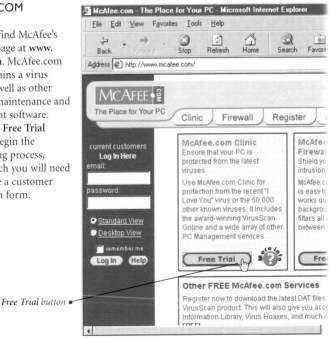

Free Trial button ●

NORTON ANTIVIRUS

● This is available from Symantec's site at **www.symantec.com**. Look for links to trialware or free 30-day demo versions. The web page design may change, but the trial version will almost certainly be available to download.

● Again, you will be required to submit an online customer information form.

Symantec Protects Yahoo! Mail
May 16, 2000 in *Press Center.*

Email Monitoring: Privacy Issues
May 10, 2000 in *Enterprise Security.*

Quick Links

Product Updates   Symantec Anti
Product Upgrades   Norton Internet
Trialware   Purchasing An

om/Pages/TBYB/index.html

Shopping Cart   Order Status

Try Before You Buy
The products shown on this page provide a free 30 day trial with a purchase option.

Mobile WinFax 1.0

 Mobile WinFax provides a professional image for people on the move. Now you can send and receive high-quality faxes with your Palm Computing device.

Windows 95/98/NT
Download Now!

Norton AntiVirus 2000 6.0

 Norton AntiVirus from Symantec is the #1 anti-virus software in the world. Enjoy the security of automatic Internet and email protection plus easy updating.

Windows 95/98
Download Now!
Windows NT/2000
Download Now!

ANTIVIRAL TOOLKIT PRO

● This Swiss company produces an antivirus checker that contains 30,000 virus records, many of which can detect and disinfect multiple viruses and variants.

● Antiviral Toolkit Pro, like the other products in this section, can detect viruses in compressed and archived files. A 30-day evaluation version is available.

Metropolitan Network BBS Inc. - Swiss AVP Distribution Site - Microsoft

File   Edit   View   Favorites   Tools   Help

Back   Forward   Stop   Refresh   Home   Search   Favori

Address http://www.avp.ch/

Home   Virus Database

AVP ANTIVIRAL TOOLKIT PRO

avp.ch News

Latest antivirus definitions update posted on:
Jul-04-00 at 16:50
(W. Europe Daylight Time)
more ▸

Virus Encycl.
Newest descriptions

Welcome to www.avp.ch, the official swiss web-site of KasperskyLab's AntiViral Toolkit Pro.

NEW: Daily updates available!
Last update: 04.07.2000, 37273 records.

Test-drive AntiViral Toolkit Pro Gold today. **Download 30-day evaluation** version.

Secure Computing 5-Star rating! Read the review on

Advisory
I-Worm.
released 02

Advisory
I-Worm.
SMS mes
update rele.

Advisori
Macro.W
27.05.200
Macro.E
25.05.200

ESAFE DESKTOP

● Aladdin's eSafe Desktop antivirus suite of programs is available free of charge to home users. The antivirus part of the suite detects common viruses as well as those created in, for example, Visual Basic.

● The suite also includes internet content filtering.

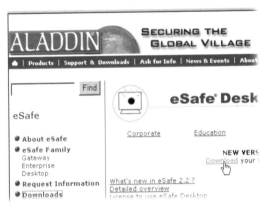

OTHER VIRUS CHECKERS

● Go to one of the major shareware sites – in this example, **www.winfiles.com** and navigate to the **Anti-Virus Utilities** area. Read the reviews, make your choice, and carefully follow the onscreen advice and instructions.

● Having downloaded the software, double-click on the appropriate **.exe** file, then follow the onscreen instructions. This should be the last time that you download a program to your computer and install it without first running a virus scan on it.

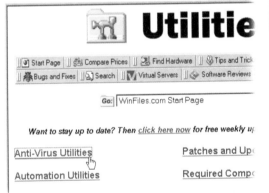

KEEP UP-TO-DATE

It is important to return frequently to the software manufacturer's site to download virus update files. These enable your virus checker to update its files and recognize – and destroy – new viruses as they appear. When a severely destructive virus appears, manufacturers usually post information and fixes on their websites very quickly.

FILE DECOMPRESSION SOFTWARE

When you download files from the internet – especially programs and large files of any kind – they will be compressed in some way. There are three reasons why files are compressed. First, in a compressed form they occupy less space on the remote server from which you can download the files. Second, they download to your computer faster. And third, compressed files can combine any number of files into a single compressed file. These files are usually called *archives*.

FILE DECOMPRESSION PROGRAMS

● As a high proportion of files that you download are likely to be compressed, a program to decompress them and restore them to their original form is an essential piece of software.

● There are many reliable file decompression programs available for downloading; they can be found by browsing the utilities area of download sites. The internet software site, **www.tucows.com**, (right) offers many decompression programs. Two of the most popular decompression programs are WinZip and PKZip.

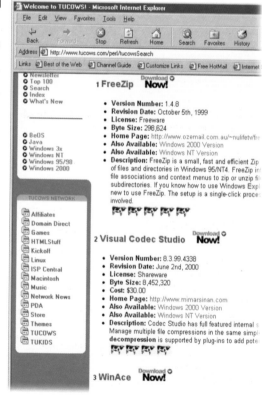

WINZIP

WinZip is available as shareware from the manufacturer's website at: **www.winzip.com** as well as from virtually all shareware sites. WinZip is capable of handling a very wide range of compressed files.

PKZIP

A decompression program, PKZip, is available from **www.pkware.com** and, like WinZip, can be used to create compressed files as well as to decompress files.

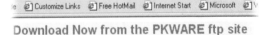

Download Now from the PKWARE ftp site

PKZIP 2.70 for Windows 95/98/2000/NT (32-bit version)

Download PKZIP 2.70 for Windows (1,067,555 bytes)*

*Note:This file contains support for advertising display via Conducent Technologies' Adgateway. For more information please see the Spons Messaging Display FAQ page.

PKZIP 2.70 is 32-bit only! If you require a 16-bit version of PKZIP for Windows 3.1x or NT 3.5, please see PKZIP 2.6

New Features in 2.70

- Create 32-bit self-extracting (Explorer enabled) Wind archives to run on Windows 9x and Windows NT (Registered and Distribution Licensed versions only)
- Embed PKWARE Authenticity Verification (AV) Information to ensure file integrity (Registered and Distribution Licensed versions only)

ad/pk270wsp.html

SELF-EXTRACTING FILES

In addition to zip files, there are also self-extracting files. These look like program files and have a **.exe** extension. All you have to do is to double-click on them and they extract themselves to your hard disk.

DOWNLOADING WINZIP FROM TUCOWS

One of the best way to check out what's available is to visit one of the main shareware download sites. This example shows Tucows, a large, well-organized shareware site that has many features in common with other major download sites.

● Go to the main Tucows page at **www.tucows.com** and click on the operating-system category that is relevant to you.

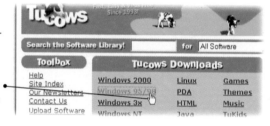

Software that is specific to your particular operating system can be found grouped together

● Choose the region nearest you from the list provided and click **Continue**.

Please select the country you live in (or the one nearest you).

Pick a Region:

Africa
Asia
Australia
Canada
Europe
Latin America & Caribbean
United States

Continue button ●————— Continue

● Choose the region nearest you by clicking in the appropriate box.

United States Region	
🌐 **AL - Huntsville** World Presence, Inc.	🌐 **Alabama** Wiregrass Communications
🌐 **Alaska** Arctic	🌐 **Alaska** Internet Alaska
🌐 **Alaska** Sinbad	🌐 **Anaheim** Internet Business Services, Inc.
🌐 **Arizona** Inficad	🌐 **Arizona** Interwork Network Services

The Tucows website contains a number of local links ●

● Navigate to the appropriate section of the site – in this case, **Compression Utilities** under **General Tools**.

● Choose **WinZip** from the list of compression utilities and click **Full Review**.

● After reading the review, click the **Download Now** button.

● The **File Download** dialog box opens. Click on the **Save this program to disk** radio button and click on **OK**.

● If the **File Download** dialog box does not appear, click on **Click Here** in the alternate window that appears.

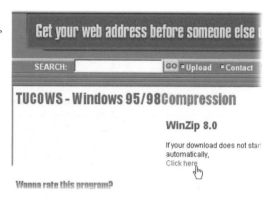

● In the **Save in** text box of the **Save As** dialog box, navigate to the **downloads** folder on your hard disk and click on **Save**.

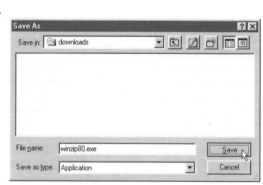

● The WinZip installer file will now download to the **downloads** folder of your computer.

● When the WinZip installer has finished downloading, the **Download complete** dialog box opens. Click the **Open Folder** button.

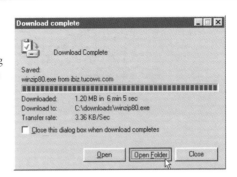

● Before you proceed with the installation, remember to run a virus checker on the newly downloaded file. The procedure will differ depending on the antivirus software on your PC, but most virus checkers can be activated by right-clicking on the file to be scanned. Try to make this checking procedure automatic every time you download a new program.

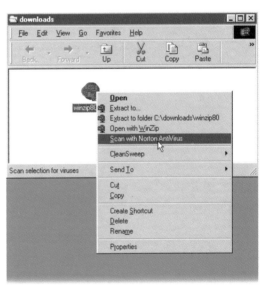

● To install WinZip, double-click the installer file in the **downloads** folder. The **WinZip Setup** dialog box opens. Click on **Setup** and carefully follow the onscreen instructions.

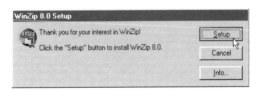

ESSENTIAL DOWNLOADS

The essential downloads are updates for your operating system, hardware drivers, and virus definitions. Some manufacturers make this procedure as easy as possible.

DOWNLOADING WINDOWS UPDATES

To guarantee the optimum efficiency of Windows 98, you should periodically use the Windows Update feature. This is an online extension of Windows 98 that automates most of the update procedure, so you simply have to answer a few simple questions and make some decisions about which elements you feel you need to download. Windows automatically checks your computer to see whether you are using the latest software components and accessories by downloading a file to your computer and then checking to see whether its contents match the components currently installed on your system. If the Windows site contains components more up-to-date than the ones installed on your computer, you'll be able to choose the relevant items on the checklist that eventually appears.

WINDOWS UPDATE SITE

● As well as updates to system files and device drivers, you will also find service packs being offered. These contain bug fixes and updates for Windows 98 and Internet Explorer, and new Windows 98 features, such as upgrades to Microsoft's Media Player, when they are available.

1 RUN WINDOWS UPDATE

● To run Windows Update, make sure that you are online, then click the **Start** button and choose **Windows Update** from the **Settings** menu.

2 PRODUCT UPDATES

● You are connected to the main page of the Microsoft Windows Update site, which provides information about the latest upgrades available for downloading. Click the **Product Updates** link.

Product Updates is one of several support options on this site

Welcome to Windows Update

The online extension of Windows that helps you get the most out of your computer. Click about Windows Update to find out more.

PRODUCT UPDATES
Go here to download and install the latest updates for your computer.

SUPPORT INFORMATION
Get help using Windows Update by reading our

3 CHECKING THE COMPONENTS

● Windows Update now attempts to check the Windows components you are using on your computer by running the Microsoft Active Setup program.

● If this is the first time you have accessed a Microsoft site and downloaded information from it, a **Security Warning** dialog box opens. Click on **Yes** to continue.

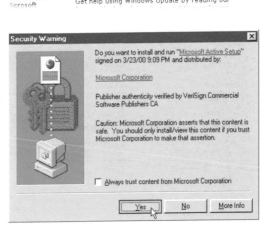

Security Warning

Do you want to install and run "Microsoft Active Setup" signed on 3/23/00 9:09 PM and distributed by:

Microsoft Corporation

Publisher authenticity verified by VeriSign Commercial Software Publishers CA

Caution: Microsoft Corporation asserts that this content is safe. You should only install/view this content if you trust Microsoft Corporation to make that assertion.

☐ Always trust content from Microsoft Corporation

Yes   No   More Info

● The components that make up the operating system on your computer are now checked against the catalog file. While this examination is taking place, the **Checking Available Updates** box appears and assures you that no information is being sent to Microsoft during this procedure.

4 COMPONENTS TO DOWNLOAD

● A **Selected Software** list appears and shows any updates, product enhancements, and new Windows 98 utilities that are not currently installed on your computer. Work your way down the list, checking the boxes next to those components you would like to download. It is highly recommended that you choose those marked as critical or security updates. Finally, click on **Download**.

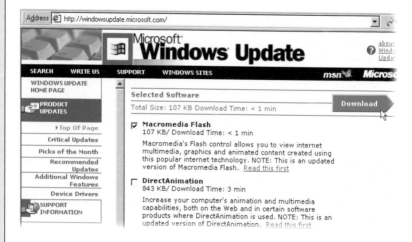

5 CHECK THE CHECKLIST

● The **Download Checklist** page opens, listing your choices and showing the size of the download and the estimated time the download will take. Here you can deselect some of these options and download them later if you are short of time. However, it is advisable to download any critical upgrades.

Product Updates

Download Checklist

1 Confirm Selections
You have chosen to install the following software. You can deselec the components you do not want to install by clearing the check b

Total Size: 107 KB Download Time: < 1 min

☑ **Macromedia Flash** 107 KB/ Download Time: < 1 min

2 View Instructions?
View a single, combined instruction page for all of the software yo chosen to install. You may want to print these instructions for later reference.

View Instructions

6 VIEW INSTRUCTIONS

● Click on the **View Instructions** button if you need to.

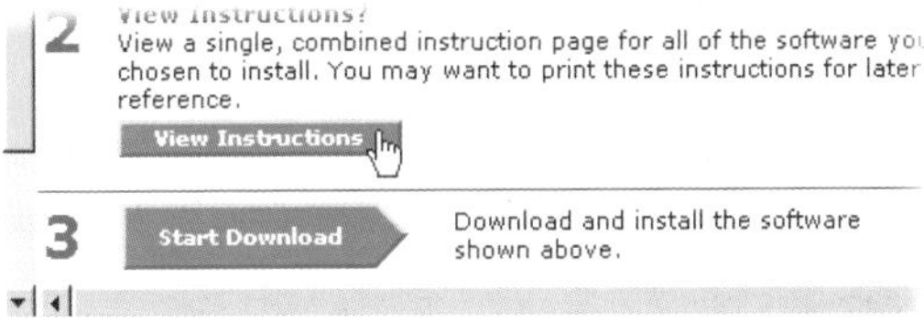

2 View Instructions?
View a single, combined instruction page for all of the software yo chosen to install. You may want to print these instructions for later reference.

View Instructions 🖑

3 Start Download ▶ Download and install the software shown above.

● The instructions screen tells you what you can do with Macromedia Flash and provides detailed instructions on how to install the files after you have downloaded them.

Macromedia Flash

Macromedia's Flash control allows you to view internet multimedia, graphics and animated content created using this popular internet technology.

Note: This is an updated version of Macromedia Flash.

How to download and install

1. On the Product Updates page, select the check box next to **Macromedia Flash**.

7 STARTING THE DOWNLOAD

● Finally, begin the downloading process by clicking on the **Start Download** button.

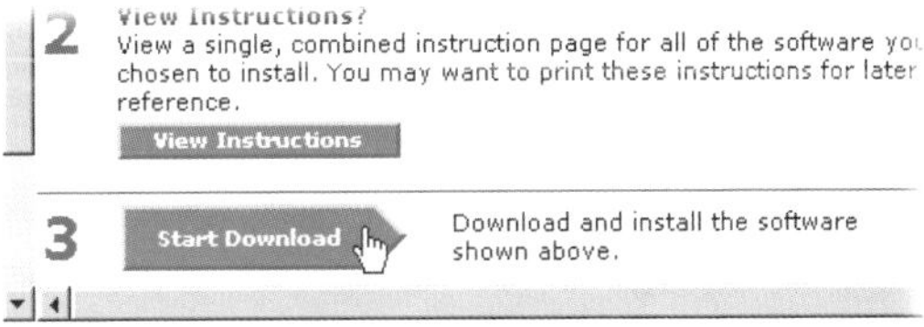

2 View Instructions?
View a single, combined instruction page for all of the software yo chosen to install. You may want to print these instructions for later reference.

View Instructions

3 Start Download 🖑 ▶ Download and install the software shown above.

● For certain downloads you may be asked to agree to a license agreement. In this example, read the contents of the **Windows Update – Web Page Dialog** box that appears and, if you agree, click on **Yes**.

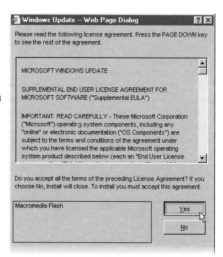

● A series of progress boxes appears, which charts the progress of your download.

● When the download is completed successfully, a panel informs you. Click the **Back** button and you will be asked to restart your computer. Click on **Yes**. This allows Windows to install the new components and upgrades.

● If you use the Windows Update option every month or so, you will not have to spend a long time downloading updates in a single session.

SUCCESSFUL

The following software was successfully downloaded and installed.
Macromedia Flash

Back

MAINTAINING YOUR VIRUS CHECKER

One of the most important routine downloads you need to make is the virus definition updates for your antivirus program. Each antivirus program has a different method for updating its virus recognition files, but nearly all manufacturers make the updated files available on their websites for customers to download. The download and installation procedure is usually very straightforward. To make things even simpler, many programs come with an auto-update option that automatically downloads these updates for you at a time that you specify – usually at least once or twice a month. If your virus checker does not include an automatic download feature, arrange your own regular reminder to check for virus updates, perhaps by using your diary or calendar.

REGULAR VIRUS CHECK

● There's no need to become obsessed with the fear of viruses. However, a regular virus check using current virus definition files, together with regular backups of your data, are both strongly recommended. The illustration shows Norton Antivirus being scheduled to do a weekly virus check.

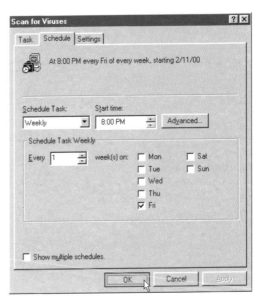

EMERGENCY DOWNLOADS

People who create computer viruses rarely bother with press releases before letting their creations loose on the world. This is as good a reason as any for checking out your antivirus program manufacturer's website regularly. But if you hear about a particularly nasty strain, (like the VBS/Newlove virus that first appeared in May 2000 and developed mutant strains for some time after), visit your antivirus manufacturer's website as soon as possible. When a new virus appears, you will usually find an emergency update to download, together with essential instructions.

● This example shows timely advice on the VBS/Newlove virus in May 2000 at McAfee.com's site at www.mcafee.com.

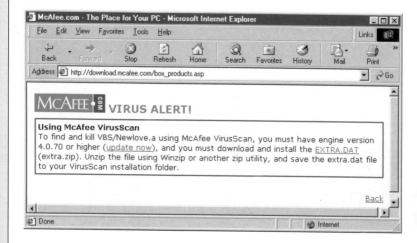

DOWNLOADING DEVICE DRIVERS

A device driver is software that enables a hardware device such as a modem or printer to interpret commands from the operating system. If your printer fails to function, the problem might not be with Windows 98. It may be a problem caused by an out-of-date or inefficient driver supplied by the printer manufacturer.

AN INFREQUENT PROBLEM

Fortunately, such software shortcomings aren't a daily occurrence unless you have serious hardware problems. So most of us don't need to worry about updating drivers until a glitch occurs. Your computer is unlikely to grind to a halt if you are not using up-to-date drivers for all your peripherals, but it is likely to perform a lot better if you do have the latest drivers on board.

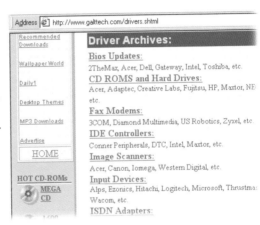

Address http://www.galttech.com/drivers.shtml

Recommended Downloads
Wallpaper World
Daily1
Desktop Themes
MP3 Downloads
Advertise
HOME

HOT CD-ROMs
MEGA CD

Driver Archives:

Bios Updates:
2TheMax, Acer, Dell, Gateway, Intel, Toshiba, etc.
CD ROMS and Hard Drives:
Acer, Adaptec, Creative Labs, Fujitsu, HP, Maxtor, NE etc.
Fax Modems:
3COM, Diamond Multimedia, US Robotics, Zyxel, etc.
IDE Controllers:
Conner Peripherals, DTC, Intel, Maxtor, etc.
Image Scanners:
Acer, Canon, Iomega, Western Digital, etc.
Input Devices:
Alps, Ezonics, Hitachi, Logitech, Microsoft, Thrustma: Wacom, etc.
ISDN Adapters:

When to look

Unlike checking for virus definition lists, you don't need to look for device drivers on a very regular, routine basis. You are most likely to download and install new drivers after experiencing a problem. Often, the manufacturer's technical support staff for the affected equipment will advise you to "go to our Web/FTP site and download a driver called ourdriver.exe." Be sure to follow the manufacturer's instructions. The more professional a supplier is, the better the advice you'll receive online, and the easier the process will be.

WHERE TO LOOK

● If you can't find the manufacturer's site, there are many websites specifically devoted to drivers that are worth a visit. This example shows the **windrivers.com** site, which provides a very wide range of Windows drivers along with extensive online help on how to download and install them. The site includes identification features for your hardware, including search and "identify by photograph" options.

BE PREPARED

You will need to know the make and model of your hardware before looking for drivers on websites. If you can't find the details stamped on the equipment case, read the manuals, the readme files that were installed with the accompanying software, or – failing all else – call the supplier with your sales invoice on hand and ask for advice.

Beginners Search At WinDrivers.com - Microsoft Internet Explorer

File   Edit   View   Favorites   Tools   Help

Address 🔗 http://www.windrivers.com/BEGINNER/index.htm

Free WinDrivers Newsletter!
Are You On The List?
| | SignUp! |

Make WinDrivers My Start Page

Xdrive Backup You
click here

WinDrivers.co
The #1 Resource for Windows

HOME | Auctions | Computer Classifieds | Free Email | Up To 100MB Free Storage |

Driver Center
Advanced Search
Beginner Search
Driver Installation Help
Driver Updates

Tech Support
3D Video
AMD Athlon Center
Anti-Virus Center
Bus Mastering
Certification
DLL Files
DVD Software Center
Exception Errors
Hard Drive Center
Hardware Reviews
Identify Hardware
Memory Center
Modem Help Center
MS Support/Fixes
Service Packs
Tech Tips
Troubleshooting
Tutorial Center
Tech Tools/Utilities

Forum Center
Forum Center
Post or find the answer to all your questions in the company & support forums or search over 20 different computer forums across the net.

General/Fun
About Us
Awards
Contact
Link To Us
Computer Humor
Trivia Break
User's Guide
Windows Timeline

Finding Your Driver

Welcome to WinDrivers.com, we'll help you get th
and better than any other site! Just follow these

If you don't know what a driver is, you can read t
you up to speed:

Drivers Ed:
The Beginner's Guide to D

Driver's Ed: The Beginner's Guide

What you will need to know to start y

Manufacturer Name

Who made my Product? i.e. Creative Labs

Don't know the manufacturer, Click Here for t

Another search method if your component is a N
Network Adapter, Sound Card or Video Card, the
specialized search for the manufacturer by going

Identification by Photo/Model

Model Name

What is the Product name?
i.e. SoundBlaster AWE32

Operating System

What operating system am I running?
i.e. DOS, Windows 3.1, Windows 95, Windows 98

Product Category

What type of component do I have?
i.e. BIOS, CD-ROM/CDR, Hard Drive, IDE Control
Monitor, Network Card, Notebook, Printer, Plotte
Adapter, Scanner, Sound Card, Tape Backup, US

The more information you have the easier it
Once you have your information, continue on

MODEM SUPPORT

● 3Com's website makes it easy for their customers to find the latest drivers for their modems.

● Any well-designed website will make it easy for you to locate the software that you want. Here, clicking on **Modems** brings up the 3Com **Modem Support** page.

BETTER SAFE THAN SORRY

It is possible to overwrite important Windows 98 files when installing a driver. Before installing, it is worth backing up all Windows 98 folders and subfolders. If in doubt, don't do it. Ask for advice from the product supplier or the technical support service of your computer supplier.

● *From this page, you can access upgrades, updates, driver files, and documentation relating to the company's range of modems*

DOWNLOADING PLUG-INS

Plug-ins are third-party programs that handle video, audio, animation, games, and interactive documents. When your web browser encounters a file that it cannot display or launch, you are usually invited to download the required plug-in. This will inevitably happen for plug-ins that are already installed on your computer since enhancements are constantly being developed and launched.

REALPLAYER
RealPlayer is a plug-in with which you can listen to audio and view video content on the web, including streaming MP3 and approximately 2500 internet radio stations.

WHAT IS ACTIVEX?

Similar to plug-ins, Microsoft's ActiveX controls enhance Internet Explorer's multimedia capabilities. When you encounter a page that uses an ActiveX control, you will be invited to download it to your hard disk where it will install and configure itself automatically. The control then becomes active each time it is required on a web page, launching the relevant program or file.

HOW TO INSTALL REALPLAYER
● To install the RealPlayer plug-in, go to the manufacturer's site at **www.realplayer.com** and follow the links to the free RealPlayer page. Downloading from this site guarantees that you will be downloading the latest version of the software. When you have reached the appropriate page, click the RealPlayer download button (in this example, the **RealPlayer 8 Basic beta** button).

Selecting RealPlayer ●

● A new page appears containing the RealPlayer download form. Use the drop-down menus on this page to specify your operating system (Windows 98), computer processor, language, and modem type. Then click the **Download FREE RealPlayer 8 Basic beta** button.

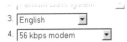

3. English

4. 56 kbps modem

5. **1¢/Minute Phone Calls Over the Internet!** Use Net2Phone to make phone calls to anywhere in the US from your PC and recei FREE high quality telephone headset!

☐ Bundle Net2Phone with my free RealPlayer. *Net2Phone activation requires a $9.95 credit card pre-payment.*

Choosing Net2Phone will give you Real Entertainment Center Basic Complete which also includes RealJukebox, RealDownload and AOL Instant Messenger rates, promotional or otherwise, are subject to change without notice. This is a limited time offer for new customers residing in the U.S. and may not be comb with any other offer.

6. ☑ Notify me of important news about RealNetworks consumer products and special offers.

| Download FREE RealPlayer 8 Basic beta |

Download RealPlayer

● The next part of the download form gives you a choice of Complete, Standard, or Minimal download options, with a useful indication of how long each download should take using a 56K modem. Click the appropriate radio button and click the **Download FREE RealPlayer Basic Now** button.

You may choose to download RealPlayer as a standalone application or as a part of the new Real Entertainment Center, your internet media suite.

Features Include:	Real Entertainment Center Complete	Real Entertainment Center Standard	RealPlayer Basic Standalone
RealPlayer Basic - Play Streaming Audio & Video	✓	✓	✓
RealJukebox Basic - Digital Music, CD Recording, MP3s	✓	✓	
RealDownload Basic - Internet Download Manager	✓	✓	
AOL Instant Messenger	✓		
Net2Phone - Make calls from your PC for just $0.01/minute!	✓		
Make Your Selection	○	⊙ Recommended	○

| Download FREE RealPlayer Basic Now |

Currently beta software

Real Entertainment Center Basic Complete Download: 13.6 MB
Real Entertainment Center Basic Standard Download: 9.2 MB
RealPlayer Standalone Download: 4.2 MB

● The next part of the download form invites you to choose the server nearest to your location. Click the appropriate server location.

1. Verify that you have selected the correct version of the product for the operating system you are using.

2. Click on a location near you to begin downloading (Size: 9 MB):

Seattle, WA Seattle, WA Seattle, WA	Paris, France Amsterdam, Netherlands Frankfurt am Main	Osaka, Japan Melbourne, VIC Australia

● After a few seconds, a **File Download** dialog box opens. Click on the **Save this program to disk** radio button and click on **OK**.

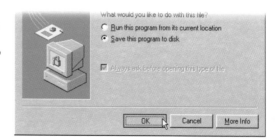

What would you like to do with this file?

○ _R_un this program from its current location
● _S_ave this program to disk

☑ Always ask before opening this type of file

[OK]   [Cancel]   [More Info]

● The program now downloads to your computer, and a progress bar monitors the download.

5% of rec-setup.exe Completed

Saving:
rec-setup.exe from 205.158.7.40

Estimated time left: 47 min 10 sec (439 KB of 9.00 MB copied)
Download to: C:\downloads\Programs\rec-setup.exe
Transfer rate: 3.38 KB/Sec

☐ Close this dialog box when download completes

[Open]   [Open Folder]   [Cancel]

BE PREPARED TO SWAP SERVERS

If the download speed appears to be painfully slow – even though you have chosen the server nearest to you from the list provided – cancel the download by clicking **Cancel** in the File Download window and returning to the list of download sites. Then simply try another server, or servers, until you find one with an acceptable download speed.

LOOKING FOR PLUG-INS

You do not normally need to look for plug-ins. Usually they announce their presence the moment you arrive on a web page that requires you to have one installed. In such cases, downloading and installing are made as easy as possible for you by the software manufacturers.

LIMITED-USE PLUG-INS

Some plug-ins may provide wonderful browser-enhancing experiences, but only on a handful of websites! If you are not convinced that you will be returning to such a site (and don't want to devote a lot of download time for that reason) click the **Cancel** button or view the site with the graphics switched off. You don't have to accept every plug-in that is offered!

● For collections of plug-ins, organized by platform, browser compatibility, and category, you can visit Internet.com's Browser-Watch Plug-in Plaza, which is one of many excellent shareware download sites that are dedicated simply to plug-ins.

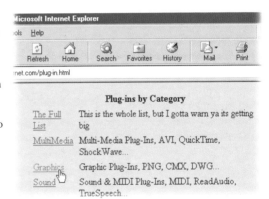

Plug-ins by Category

The Full List	This is the whole list, but I gotta warn ya its getting big
MultiMedia	Multi-Media Plug-Ins, AVI, QuickTime, ShockWave...
Graphics	Graphic Plug-Ins, PNG, CMX, DWG...
Sound	Sound & MIDI Plug-Ins, MIDI, ReadAudio, TrueSpeech...

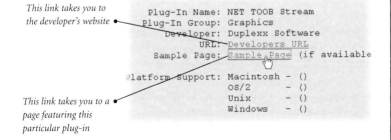

This link takes you to the developer's website

```
   Plug-In Name: NET TOOB Stream
  Plug-In Group: Graphics
      Developer: Duplexx Software
            URL: Developers URL
    Sample Page: Sample Page (if available
```

This link takes you to a page featuring this particular plug-in

```
Platform Support: Macintosh - ()
                  OS/2      - ()
                  Unix      - ()
                  Windows   - ()
```

EXPLORER'S CACHE

During downloading, it is easy to overlook how much
background work the web browser is doing – downloading
words, images, sound files, and other web page elements.

TEMPORARY INTERNET FILES

When Internet Explorer accesses a web
page, it doesn't only display the page; it
also downloads information including
that page's HTML source code, images,
and other components into a folder on
your hard disk known as the browser
cache. The next time you access that web
page, your browser loads files from the
cache folder, which is much faster than
downloading the files from the website.
For a web page to qualify for inclusion in
the browser cache, you must first let the
page load fully while you are online
before moving to another page.

VIEW THE CONTENTS
OF THE WEB CACHE

● Internet Explorer's cache
folder (called **Temporary
Internet Files**) is stored in
the **Windows** folder. You
can view the contents using
Windows Explorer, but if
you double-click on one of
these files, a message warns
you that opening them
might cause problems
when you next use your
internet browser.

● The contents of this
folder are images that
appear on the web page
www.procreative.co.uk

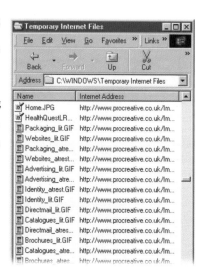

VIEWING WEB PAGES OFFLINE

There are two reasons for viewing web pages offline. First, your browser will load copies of the most recently visited pages faster from the cache than by accessing them "live" via your modem. Second, you can view web pages offline when you are not connected to the internet – ideal if you are using a laptop PC while traveling.

1 SELECT WORKING OFFLINE

● With your web browser running, click on the **File** menu and select **Work Offline**.

2 SELECTING THE WEB PAGE

● There are two ways to select the page. You can choose an entry from your **Favorites** menu – the pages stored in the cache are listed in bold type.
● Alternatively, if you know the website address of the page stored in the cache, you can type it in the browser's address bar and press Enter↵. The page is read from memory and appears immediately.

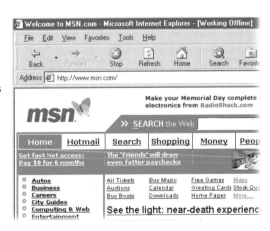

CHANGING YOUR CACHE SETTINGS

When you visit a web page, its contents are added automatically to the browser cache. When the cache is full, the sites with the earliest date are deleted as new pages are added. However, you have some control over how the cache works. First, you can decide how large the **Temporary Internet Folder** is to be. Second, you can nominate particular websites for inclusion and updating in the cache.

1 SELECT INTERNET OPTIONS

● To create more space for temporary internet pages, click **Internet Options** on the **Tools** menu.

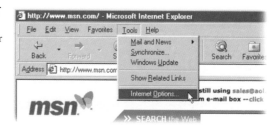

2 SELECTING SETTINGS

● The **Internet Options** dialog box opens. On the **General** tab, click **Settings** in the **Temporary Internet files section**.

Exclusions from the cache

Some page elements, such as database entries in online shopping catalogs, are not made available offline. But you can view most web pages offline provided that you have visited the page before.

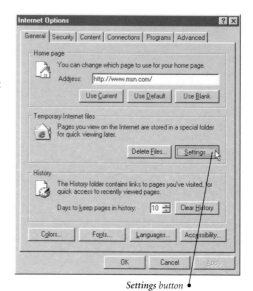

Settings button ●

3 UPDATING A PAGE

● To ensure that you are seeing the latest version of a web page, Internet Explorer can check for updated pages when you are online. Clicking the **Every visit to the page** radio button means that Internet Explorer will check whether this page has changed since you last viewed it. If it is newer, it will overwrite the version stored in the cache.

4 INCREASING AVAILABLE SPACE

● If you are likely to do much offline browsing, make the amount of space available for the **Temporary Internet Files** folder as large as possible.

● In the **Settings** dialog box, increase the amount of space available for the browser cache by moving the slider to the right. Then click on **OK**.

DOWNLOADING WEB PAGE ELEMENTS

The following few examples show how you can download parts of web pages while viewing them online and saving them to an appropriate area of your hard disk. It is also possible to return to these pages offline and save the images and text using the same methods, but only if the pages have been correctly cached ⌐.

SAVING IMAGES

● To save images from a web page, right-click the image and choose **Save Picture As** from the pop-up menu.

Copyright matters
Remember to observe the copyright laws for words, images, or anything else you save from the internet and intend to reuse.

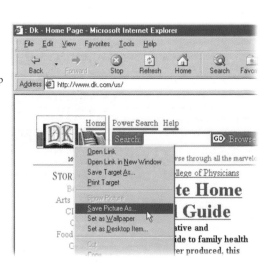

● In the **Save Picture** dialog box, navigate to a suitable folder. In this example, a folder called **web images** has been created in the **downloads** folder for this purpose. If required, choose a new name for the image by overtyping the original name in the **File name** box. Then click on **Save**.

● The extracted and saved image can then be viewed in almost any image editing program.

DOWNLOADING TEXT

● You can copy and paste text from any web page into a word processing program. To do this highlight the text you want to copy by dragging the mouse cursor over the required area so that it is highlighted.

● Right-click over the highlighted area and choose **Copy** from the pop-up menu.

● Open your preferred word-editing program – this example shows Wordpad. Right-click anywhere on the editing window and choose **Paste** from the pop-up menu.

● The text will now appear on the page and can be used and saved as appropriate.

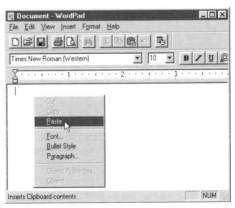

DOWNLOADING AN ENTIRE WEB PAGE

● To download an entire web page, display the page and choose **Save As** from the **File** menu.

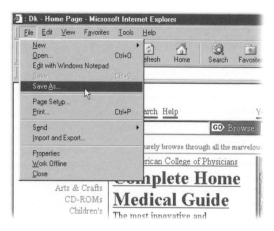

● Navigate to an appropriate folder on your hard disk. This example uses a specially created folder called **web pages** in the **downloads** folder.

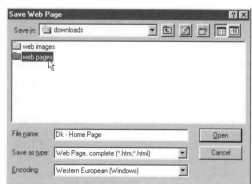

● In the **Save as type** box, select **Web Page, complete** (*.htm, *.html). Then click on **Save**.

● The **Web Page, complete** (*.htm, *.html) option saves the web page in two parts. The first is the HTML file. The second is a folder (with the same name as the HTML page) filled with the images and other files related to it.

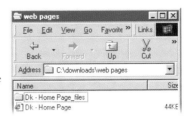

● When you double-click on the HTML file, (with an Internet Explorer icon next to it), the file appears onscreen as it would when you're online, However, the links on this page to other web pages can only be displayed offline if you have saved those pages as well.

SYNCHRONIZING WEBSITE DOWNLOADS

To make the most of Internet Explorer's offline browsing capability, you need to use the synchronized downloads feature. This enables you to specify that a particular web page (or collection of web pages) is saved to your browser cache and then updated at regular intervals. The feature is highly customizable and can be accessed by several different routes. The examples here show how to apply synchronized downloading to the web pages that appear in your **Favorites** menu.

● In Internet Explorer, choose **Organize Favorites** from the **Favorites** menu.

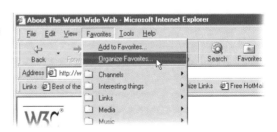

● In the **Organize Favorites** dialog box, highlight the web page you intend to make available for synchronized updates and check the **Make available offline** box.

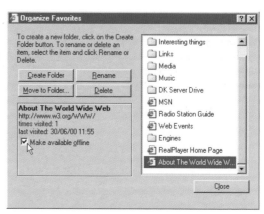

● Click the **Properties** button that appears after you have checked the **Make available offline** check box.

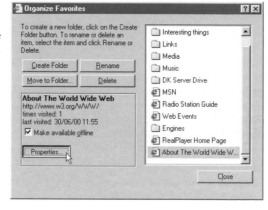

NUMBER OF LINKS DEEP

Take care not to set too high a figure when setting the number of **links deep from this page**. Two links deep means that all pages linked to your chosen page will be saved, and then the same will apply to all the secondary links. You could fill a lot of hard disk space with data that you may not need.

● In the **Properties** dialog box of the web page that you are organizing, click on the **Download** tab. Here you can specify the number of links deep from this page to download (see box featured opposite).

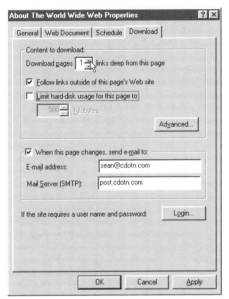

● You are offered a **Limit hard disk usage for this page to:** option, to limit the disk allocation for this page.

● If you want to be informed every time the content of this page changes, use the **send e-mail to:** feature offered here. Check the **When this page changes, send e-mail to:** box and fill in your email and mail server addresses in the boxes provided.

● Click on the **Advanced** button for more download options.

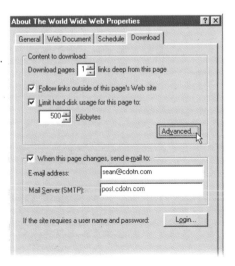

● In the **Advanced Download Options** dialog box, use the check boxes to specify whether images or other multimedia elements are to be downloaded for that page.

● Having made the selections, click on **OK** to close this box.

● Click on **OK** to close the **Properties** box of the web page.

● You are returned to the **Organize Favorites** dialog box. Click on **OK**.

● The **Synchronizing** box appears showing how far the synchronizing has progressed.

● The **Synchronizing Complete** box briefly appears when the process is complete, and you are returned to your browser window.

SYNCHRONIZING MANUALLY

● When you have specified a web page for synchronization, you can bring its stored contents up to date by first choosing **Synchronize** from the browser's **Tools** menu.

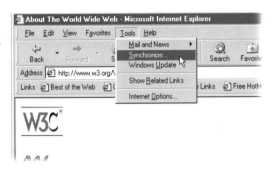

● In the **Items to Synchronize** dialog box, check the boxes for the appropriate items and then click the **Synchronize** button.

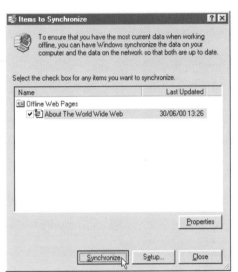

● The **Synchronizing** dialog box shows the progress of the download. When the process is complete the **Synchronizing Complete** dialog box briefly appears, and you are returned to the browser.

DOWNLOAD SITES

This chapter describes the different types of download sites available on the web – from the comprehensive to the specialist – and suggests how you can get the most from them.

SITE FEATURES

A quick look at the main page of a site like completelyfreesoftware.com (**www.completelyfreesoftware.com**) gives an accurate snapshot of the scale and scope of the downloads that the major download sites offer (see pages 68–69 for a selective list of major download sites). They are usually extremely well organized, making it easy to find the area you wish to explore. Each site does things differently, however, and you will soon find that you

prefer the feel of one site over another in the same way that you probably prefer one search engine over the others. Nevertheless, you will usually end up visiting a number of the big sites when browsing for a particular download because the completely "comprehensive" site has yet to be built. For this reason, the best download sites, either the general or the specialized sites, add features to encourage you to return and use the service.

DOWNLOAD FEATURES

These features are typically:
● Free newsletters informing you of new arrivals in the areas that interest you.
● A product-review service for new additions to the site.
● General download information including download times, size, and system requirements.
● Shown right is **www. completelyfreesoftware.com**

Windows 9x	Win 3.1/DOS	General
Desktop Utilities	Desktop Utilities	News
Games	Games	New Additions
General Apps.	General Apps.	Submit software
Graphics	Internet	Link to Us
Internet	Win Extras	CD-ROM Info
Multimedia		Various Resour
Text		WebAuthor Free
Win Extras		Free Newsletter
		Advertise with u
		Guesthook

FREE NEWSLETTERS

● Check any of the boxes below Free Newsletters on the Jumbo.com home page (**www.jumbo.com**), supply your email address, and click the **Get It** button to receive a free newsletter on the subject you have requested.

Check boxes to select newsletters ●

● Stroud's Consummate Winsock Applications List (**cws.internet.com**) is another well-established download site specializing in Windows downloads. A daily or weekly newsletter is available on the latest additions to the site.

PRODUCT REVIEWS

CNET's Download.com site (**www.download.com**) offers a good example of a site with an excellent reviews section written by the company's own staff, which is supplemented by reviews from site visitors.

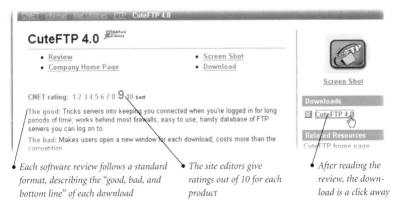

Each software review follows a standard format, describing the "good, bad, and bottom line" of each download

The site editors give ratings out of 10 for each product

After reading the review, the download is a click away

DOWNLOAD INFORMATION

● When you have decided to download a file, you are usually presented with essential information relating to the file including the size and estimated time of the download. This example from the massive download library of ZDNet (**www.zdnet.com/downloads**) contains reviews written in-house and by users of the software. It also offers a shopping basket feature that lets you choose several downloads as you browse through the site, review the contents of the basket, and choose to download all or some of the basket contents at any time.

Size of download ● *System requirements* ● ● *License information (i.e., shareware, free to try, $25 if you decide to keep it)*

DOWNLOAD SITE STRUCTURE

Softseek (**www.softseek. com**) is typical of large download sites that offer features that have become almost standard. It offers links to collections of shareware, freeware, and the latest evaluation software from commercial software developers.

Links to the category headings under which the programs and other files are organized •

Links to new releases, lists of the most frequently downloaded software, and the editor's recommended selections •

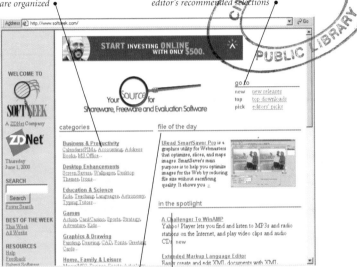

*Each day, a new piece of software is reviewed as **file of the day*** •

• *The **In the spotlight** section features new software or notable updates to existing feature*

TWO MORE DOWNLOAD SITES

Two further download sites are **wugnet.com** and **sharewarejunkies.com**. *Wugnet provides:*
● Descriptive articles of programs.
● Interface screen shots.

● Best shareware available in the Wugnet Shareware Hall of Fame. *Sharewarejunkies offers:*
● Tests of the programs that are available.
● Links to worldwide

shareware sites.
● Immense archive of programs.
● Software for many operating systems.
● An information page on a selected program.

REVIEWS YOU CAN TRUST?

● Product reviews can be written by the site's producers or by its users. That could be you, if you feel strongly enough to share your opinions with other site users.

● On some screens of Download.com (**www.download.com**) you are asked if you would recommend a product. Check the appropriate radio button and click **Submit**, in this example.

● Some sites like the MP3 HitSession. com (**www.hitsession.com**) site make a point of the fact that they do not publish professional reviewers, but only from amateur enthusiasts – just like most of us in fact.

● You can also air your views by using the newsletters related to download sites, and by submitting articles or emails to the newsgroups and to bulletin boards related to products and software manufacturers. When looking for new software, it's a case of downloader beware!

SHAREWARE AND FREEWARE SPECIALISTS

Many websites specialize in shareware and freeware ⌐. The sites that review and store (or provide shortcuts to) shareware can be as well organized and as sharply designed as any of the more general software download sites.

SAFE DOWNLOADING

● Some shareware sites have archives containing software dating from when easy-to-follow installers were not the norm. You had to be careful about running an installer as it would place its contents in the current directory rather than asking you where to install it. This is rare now, but it is worth being aware of when using more elderly downloads.

● Check the information about a program before downloading it. Use sites that offer information about the program's author, check the company's home page and the support offered. With so much shareware on offer you can shop around. Use one that gives you as much inform-ation as possible and provides accurate and up-to-date reviews.

Want to stay up to date? Then click here now for free weekly updates from WinFiles.com!

VistaWrite

Version 2.0				Online Registration Not Yet Available	
27-May-00	2,254K	Win 95/98/NT	Shareware $39.95	Expires after 30 Days	Install & Uninstall
14 min at 28.8K		5 min at 56K		2 min at ISDN 128K	

A flexible system of journal(s) and notebooks for organizing all types of personal writing. The software combines a full featured writing program with powerful search and tracking features making it a complete solution for organizing all your personal writings. VistaWrite is easy to use, secure, and includes extensive user options for creating a more personal place to write

Published by Digital Writing   VistaWrite Home Page

Diary Holder

Version 3.0				No Registration Required	
12-Apr-00	1,988K	Win 95/98/NT	Freeware	Never Expires	Install & Uninstall
12 min at 28.8K		4 min at 56K		2 min at ISDN 128K	

A program that enable you to write your special moments, diary, or anything in a nice way. This program is highly encpted that will make sure that your data will never be read by others in any way

Published by Mark Joya   Diary Holder Home Page

Plan-It

Version 1.20				Online Registration Not Yet Available	
07-Apr-00	909K	Win 95/98/NT	Shareware $45.00	Expiration Unknown	Install & Uninstall
6 min at 28.8K		2 min at 56K		2 min at ISDN 128K	

A networked diary that is geared towards users, that is, every entry is owned by, and can be assigned to users. Plan-It was designed to make it easy to view information on specific users, and contains a clever filter mechanism that allows the user to only display the users that they are interested in.

Published by MH Software   Plan-It Home Page

Loki Diary

Version 1.30				Register Now	
03-Mar-00	5,750K	Win 95/98/NT	Shareware $20.00	Expires after 60 Days	Install & Uninstall
36 min at 28.8K		13 min at 56K		6 min at ISDN 128K	

Feature packed yet easy to use Diary / Journal application. Complete with spell check, full text searching, printing, and security (encyption and password protection) Loki Diary provides navigational features which make keeping track of your diary entries as easy as one click of the mouse.

Published by Ross A. Goldberg   Loki Diary Home Page

Log Book

Version 3.0.0				Online Registration Not Yet Available	
30-Jan-00	4,102K	Win 95/98/NT	Shareware $14.00	Expiration Unknown	Install & Uninstall
26 min at 28.8K		9 min at 56K		5 min at ISDN 128K	

An enhanced Log Manager with a built in encryption engine Keep logs, journals or diaries, record your memories, search for any word in the Log Book, spell

⌐ Internet

⌐ What are the
56 different "wares"?

TIME-LIMITED COMMERCIAL DEMOS

Software developers have recently begun to offer full-featured versions of their programs that time-out after a 30-day trial period. This enables you to download a fully functional version of a program such as Macromedia's Dream-weaver from a download site or directly from the manufacturer. Some good value, try-before-you-buy deals are available, but the download times can be lengthy, so you might want to do some research in advance. Check out the recent internet magazines. They often carry the latest demo software and many of the most popular demos on the cover CDs.

WHAT ARE THE DIFFERENT "WARES"?

● Shareware is software that is free to try for a limited period, after which you should pay up or stop using it. Shareware often times itself out at the end of the trial period (typically 30 days).

● Freeware is software that you can keep and use, but it is protected by copyright.

● Public domain software is free; it may also be altered and used for profit, but the author has to state that it is public domain.

● Other variants exist including postcardware, in which the author only requests that you send him or her a postcard.

● For more information on shareware, and for an excellent collection of downloadable software, visit the Association of Shareware Professionals website at **www.asp.com**.

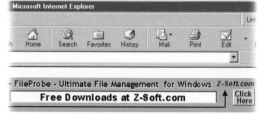

ASP — **Association of Shareware Professionals**

s the **Association of Shareware** ssionals? Read our Mission Statement and utl Also view a short Bio on the ASP as well nformational note that highlights different s of the ASP.

Find out about PAD and how it wi help revolutionize the world of Shareware distribution!

great discounts from our members. Take age of discounts from many of our ers and others involved in the Shareware ry. But don't forget, you have to be a er first. ;-)

SEARCHING FOR DOWNLOADS

Browsing through the download sites can be fun – if you have plenty of time on your hands, and if you can exercise the necessary discipline eventually to log off without downloading at least ten times more files than you will ever use.

FINDING THE SOFTWARE

● But what if you know precisely what you are looking for? By name, even? Fortunately most download sites have excellent search facilities – as shown in the Tucows site illustrated here (**www.tucows.com**). This enables you to get straight to the area holding the types of files you require or, if you have made a specific request, directly to the file that you have named.

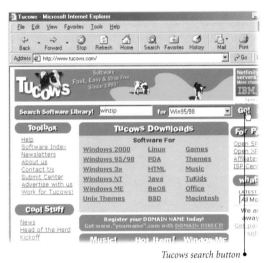

Tucows search button ●

Searching the web
For further information on how you can get the most from web directories and search engines, see *Searching the Internet*, available now in this *DK Essential Computers* series.

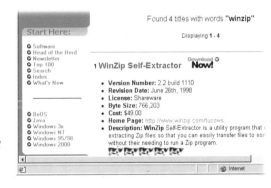

WIDENING YOUR SEARCH

● Of course, there is no need to limit yourself specifically to one search site. Many search engines allow specialized searches for particular types of software, file formats, or even simply for downloads. Many web directories and search engines now have a special search feature for audio files. The AltaVista search engine, for example, has an MP3/audio option with a number of check boxes enabling you to refine your search further. As two examples of specialist music sites for heavy metal and punk, try **www.metalseek.com** and **www.punkseek.com**.

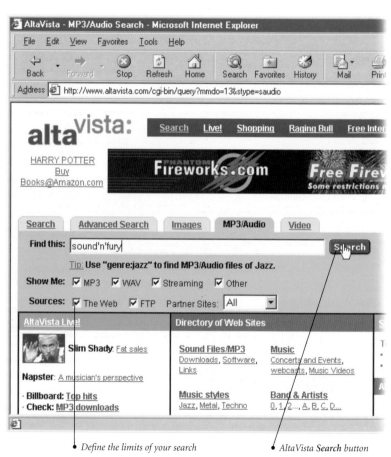

• Define the limits of your search　　　*• AltaVista **Search** button*

SPECIALIST DOWNLOAD SITES

There are very few types of download that are not covered by the general download sites. For certain kinds of information and software, however, specialist sites may well be your best first port of call. Their main advantage is a concentration of specialist information on the same site, along with many invaluable links to other sites of a similar nature. You will also find that many specialist sites compare favorably with the best of the general download sites in terms of organization and ease of use.

GAMES

● Computer games are as old as the PC itself, and have always been well represented on the internet. Some of the oldest download sites specialize in electronic games. They contain mostly commercial demos from the most up-to-date games from the leading software houses, shareware games of all levels of complexity, and massive archives of games from when space was first invaded. Somewhere out there, as you read this, a retro games fan is downloading Burger Time or PacMan, possibly from a site such as **www. gamesdomain. co.uk**, which is shown here.

GAMESDOMAIN

In addition to download areas for game demos, GamesDomain also has an area for patches and game improvements. Like many of the best specialist games sites, GamesDomain is more like an ezine than a download site, carrying news, game hints and cheats, reviews, and desktop themes. Games are organized according to operating system.

CHECK THE FILE SIZE

Be sure to note the file size before downloading game demos. Some demos can be more than 100Mb. A file of this size will easily take several hours to download using a 56k modem and it is not a viable option to consider downloading them with a slower modem. If you find yourself in the position where you simply cannot wait to get your hands on a particular demo, have a look at the free CDs attached to the covers of computer games magazines. In addition to the utilities and application demos, you may find precisely the game that you're looking for.

DEMOLAND

www.demoland.com specializes in the playable commercial demo – offering games across a wide range of categories from action to puzzles. The simple format of the site provides descriptions, screenshots, and download buttons that usually include a link to take you directly to the manufacturer's site. Some of the demos are extremely large, though, so check the details closely before embarking on a lengthy download.

MUSIC DOWNLOADS ON THE WEB

Digital music on the internet is currently going through a boom period. One of the reasons for this is the huge popularity of MP3 (MPEG-3) – a compressed audio format that can cram an entire music CD into less than 30Mb of hard disk space. This makes it an extremely popular file format both for downloading from, and for emailing across, the internet. The popularity and portability of MP3 files make it the subject of considerable ongoing debate in the recording industry.

THE USES OF SOUND

● The internet used to contain sites devoted to sound clips for downloading and using with system events on your PC. For a while, William Shatner's voice could be heard everywhere whenever a Recycle Bin was emptied or a floppy disk accessed.

● Sound files are now downloaded in live streams as PCs are used to tune into live radio broadcasts. The web is alive with the sound of MP3, and the ease of access is raising serious concerns over copyright in some quarters.

● PCs can now play and record in many audio formats, including radio broadcasts and audio CDs. Download sites are full of software to make this possible and also contain links to live audio feeds.

music4free.com contains a powerful search engine.

www.free-music.com is a musical cornucopia.

MP3
SPECIALIST SITES

The best way to keep up with these fast-changing developments is to use specialist sites, although most of the online PC magazines and general download sites also have special MP3 areas. One of the most popular specialist sites is MP3Yes.com (**www.mp3yes.com**), which has an ezine format containing news, links to the latest, essential, and popular downloads, and useful background information on the current legal situation. It contains reviews, the hottest new utilities, articles about the new technology, and links to search engines and web directories. This site gives you its own web search engine and another that enables you to access AltaVista's MP3/audio search.

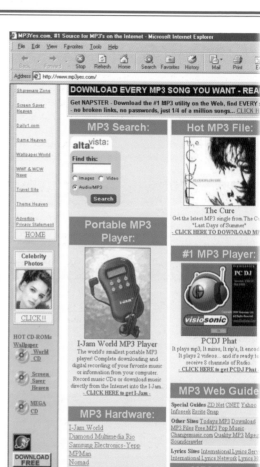

AUDIO PLAYERS

MP3 is by no means the only audio format available on the internet, so it is worth looking for a player that can handle as many of these different formats as possible. One of the most widely used software players for audio and video files on the internet is Real Jukebox (available from Real.com's site at www.real.com). This offers a wide range of multimedia facilities including playing, organizing, and searching for MP3 files. It also provides a large selection of links to relevant websites.

However, you can visit any of the download sites (specialist or general) to find a vast collection of audio players, recorders, audio file managers, and software for recording everything from the spoken word to live internet radio broadcasts.

USING FTP

FTP (File Transfer Protocol) is one of the three main protocols used on the internet, "protocol" being a language that enables computers to communicate with each other.

WHAT MAKES FTP DIFFERENT?

It is worth knowing a little about how FTP sites work since you cannot avoid encountering them at some time as an internet user. The good news is they are generally not difficult to use, and your web browser usually does all the work for you automatically if you are merely downloading files.

AN ABSENCE OF FRILLS

FTP sites are much more stripped-down, no-frills affairs than web sites, looking just like the folders and subfolders of your hard disk, as the top level of Microsoft's FTP site shows.

NAVIGATING AROUND AN FTP SITE

To navigate round an FTP site, you need to click the **Up** button in the menu bar to move up a level, or double click a folder icon to move down a level.

THE TOP-LEVEL LINKS PAGE

Well-organized FTP sites will supply a site map or an index file at the top level. Some FTP sites, like the Project Gutenberg site shown on these pages, contain a links page at the top level, which provides navigation assistance for web browser users.

Welcome to Sailor's Project Gutenberg S

- What is Project Gutenberg?
- **Project Gutenberg Electronic Texts**
  - Listings by Author
  - ○ _____ by Title

● To learn about the structure of an FTP site, look for a file called **index**, **readme**, or **site map** at the top level. Some sites provide this information within every folder. On Microsoft's FTP server, at the top level, click the file called **dirmap.htm**.

As this is an HTML file, it opens automatically in your browser window.

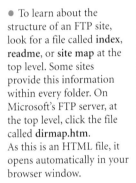

Name	Size	Type	Modified
bussys		File Folder	4/25/00 2:0
deskapps		File Folder	2/25/00 12:
developr		File Folder	2/25/00 1:3
kbhelp		File Folder	2/25/00 1:3
misc		File Folder	4/6/00 5:03
peropsys		File Folder	2/25/00 3:5
products		File Folder	2/25/00 4:0
reskit		File Folder	3/22/00 3:5
services		File Folder	2/25/00 4:2
softlib		File Folder	2/25/00 5:3
solutions		File Folder	2/25/00 5:5
dirmap.htm	7.79 KB	Microsoft HTML Doc...	1/28/99 12
dirmap.txt	4.23 KB	Text Document	1/28/99 12
disclaim1.txt	710 bytes	Text Document	4/12/93 12
disclaimer.txt	712 bytes	Text Document	9/25/94 12

This file is to help you find your way around ftp.microsoft.com. This file only covers the directory structure two levels deep. If you see a 'kb' directory in a second level directory, it contains all of the information regarding that second level directory. For example, the /developr/win32dk directory has a kb directory in it. This kb directory contains all of the articles for any 32 bit development kit.

ROOT DIRECTORY	SUB DIRECTORY	CONTENTS
BUSSYS		Business Systems
	GEN_INFO	General, non-product information
	LANMAN	LanMan & other networks
	MAIL	Mail and Schedule+
	CLIENTS	Microsoft Networking Client

WHY USE FTP SITES?

We all visit FTP sites more often than we probably notice. Download sites on the web often provide links to FTP sites at the "download this file" stage, so that we move seamlessly from HTTP to FTP when the file transfer takes place. Apart from following a hyperlink from a web page or email, the most common reason for visiting and downloading files from an FTP site is because "someone tells you to." This someone is usually a technical support person working for an Internet Service Provider, or a hardware or software supplier, who directs you to their company's FTP site. If this happens over the phone, make a note of the exact path (folder/subfolder/filename) of the file. It is better if this information arrives as part of an email because you can use the hyperlink in the message.

HOW TO ACCESS AN FTP SERVER

To access an FTP server you need to have permission from the server's administrator to access it. Most times, you will access FTP servers with the user ID of "anonymous" to indicate that you are not a regular user, but would still like access.

FTP ACCESS REQUIREMENTS

The public areas of these sites allow access to anyone, providing they log on to the server with the following information:
- user name: anonymous
- password: your email address.

Unless many people are accessing the FTP server, you should have no problems accessing the server. Servers with other log-on rules will usually make these known when you first access the site.

- Often, you need only click a website hotlink, (as this example from The Project Gutenberg website shows) and the logging-on procedure will be handled in the background by Internet Explorer.

o <u>University of Illinois</u>
  (Urbana-Champaign, Illinois)

o <u>Prairienet</u>
  (Champaign, Illinois)

o <u>Sailor's Gutenberg FTP Server</u>
  (Baltimore, Maryland)

o <u>Walnut Creek CDROM</u>
  (Silicon Valley, California)

A Project Gutenberg hotlink •

USING YOUR WEB BROWSER

● To access an FTP server with a web browser, type the server's address in the address box, but type **ftp://** instead of **http://** at the beginning of the address.

• *ftp:// denotes an FTP site*

● Most times, you will be directed to an FTP address from a hyperlink on a web page, so you won't need to type an address.
When you access an anonymous FTP server with Internet Explorer, you do not usually need to type a user name and password before being granted access because these details are sent to the server automatically. If you are not granted access immediately, or getting connected seems slow, it is likely that too many people are logged on to the server. The only answer is to find an alternative site or try to connect later.

Viruses again

Remember, regardless of how a program arrives on your computer, always check it for viruses as soon as it has finished downloading.

UPLOADING FILES TO FTP SITES

If you should need to upload files to an FTP site, you will first need to be allocated a user name and a password by the administrator of the server. If you have created your own website, for example, your Internet Service Provider will tell you how to access the area of the server that is allocated to your website. To upload your files you will probably use an FTP client program, or maybe the upload facility built into your web design program, for example, Microsoft FrontPage or Macromedia DreamWeaver.

USING FTP CLIENT PROGRAMS

If you find that you are accessing FTP servers on a very regular basis, especially to upload files, perhaps for your website, you may want to consider using an FTP client program. The programs that have proved to be the most popular are easy to install and use with the download/ upload process similar to moving files around using Windows Explorer. Once you have installed and configured the client program software, you can connect to the FTP site. You can then drag files from the remote site in the right-hand panel and drop them over the folder on your hard disk that you have in the left-hand window.

SELECTED SITES

It would take you a very long time to visit even a fraction of the download sites on the internet. To help you make the most of your time, here is a selection of the best sites.

A SITE DIRECTORY

This site directory lists some of the sites in this book, and many more. And, of course, many sites provide links to many other sites offering similar downloads. This site directory will provide you with a good jumping-off point.

GENERAL DOWNLOAD SITES

32bit.com – Home Software
http://www.32bit.com/software/

A1 Shareware Evaluations
http://www.sharewarejunkies.com/

CNET Download.com
http://www.download.com/

CWSApps – Stroud's Consummate Winsock Apps List
http://cws.internet.com/

Dave Central Shareware Archive
http://www.davecentral.com/

File Mine – Dig Our Downloads of Shareware, Games, and Commercial Demos
http://www.filemine.com/

PassTheShareware.com for shareware, freeware, freebies, games, top websites, and more
http://www.passtheshareware.com/

Welcome to the source for shareware, freeware, and evaluation software
http://www.softseek.com/

Tucows Network
http://www.tucows.com/

Welcome to WinFiles.com! The best 32-bit shareware, drivers, tips, and information on the internet!
http://www.winfiles.com/

Welcome to WinSite! The place for shareware, trialware, tips, and utilities
http://www.winsite.com/win95/

GENERAL DOWNLOAD SITES SPECIALIZING IN FREE STUFF

Totally Free Stuff
http://www.totallyfreestuff.com/

Completely FREE Software – Windows
& DOS Freeware
http://www.completelyfreesoftware.com/

Key freeware – index free software for
Windows 95 98 2000 NT
http://indigo.ie/~dermotc/index.html

Best Freeware Picks for Windows
http://www.absolutefreebies.com/freewar
epicks.html

Free-programs.com – the best freeware
on the net including, games, business,
education, and multimedia
http://www.free-programs.com/

1000 Freeware Links
http://www.mysteries-
megasite.com/freeware/freeware-1.html

GAMES AND MP3

3DFiles.Com – If you can't download it,
it ain't news
http://www.3dfiles.com/

GamesZone
http://www.gameszone.co.uk/

Welcome to the Gamers Mosh Pit!
http://www.gamersmoshpit.com/links/

Demoland!
http://www.demoland.com/

Essential Gamer – Database of PC Games
http://www.essentialgamer.com/

Daily Updated MP3 Software
http://dm.network.onlinemusic.com/site/
DMP3

Game Revolution Downloads
http://www.game-
revolution.com/download.htm

MP3Yes.com, #1 Source for MP3s on the
Internet
http://www.mp3yes.com/

BOOKS AND FAQS

Project Gutenberg Official Home Site for
light and heavy literature
http://www.gutenberg.net/

ii infinite ink internetting – 2500 FAQs
regularly posted to news groups
http://www.ii.com/internet/faqs/

1 E Books – free ebooks containing the
largest collection of classics on the net
http://www.1ebooks.com/register.shtml

Phoenix.net – internet specific links and
some links to searchable topics
http://www.phoenix.net/pdn/start/faq.html

GLOSSARY

ADSL
Asynchronous Digital Subscriber Line. An extremely fast line enabling instant web access and simultaneous telephone use.

BULLETIN BOARDS
Sites where people leave messages and advertisements.

CACHE
An area of memory, either in RAM or on the hard disk that stores frequently accessed data.

COMPRESSED FILE
A file reduced in size by replacing common patterns of data with abbreviations.

DECOMPRESSION
Restoring a compressed file to its original format.

DEVICE DRIVERS
Software enabling hardware to interpret commands from the operating system.

EZINE
An electronic magazine.

FREEWARE
Software without licensing fees or restrictions on use.

FTP SITE
An internet site where users can upload or download files.

GRAPHICS CARD
Circuitry enabling a computer to display data on its monitor.

HTML
HyperText Markup Language. The language used to create web pages with links and text formatting.

HTTP
HyperText Transfer Protocol. Used to transfer information from web servers to browsers.

HYPERLINK
A connection between one item in a document and another item in the document or in another document.

HYPERTEXT
A special database system in which text, pictures etc., are linked and accessed easily.

INTERNET SERVICE PROVIDER (ISP)
A company through which the internet is accessed by using their computers permanently connected to the net.

ISDN
Integrated Services Digital Network. A connection with high data transfer speeds.

MEGAHERTZ
A measure of frequency equivalent to one million cycles per second.

MEMORY
A device in a computer where information can be temporarily or permanently stored and retrieved.

MODEM
A device allowing your computer to communicate with another computer over phone lines.

MP3
An audio file format that can compress a music CD into less than 30Mb.

PATCH
A modification of a program, which is often a temporary fix.

PLUG-IN
An accessory program that enhances a main application, such as a web browser giving it special capabilities, particularly for multimedia websites.

SELF-EXTRACTING FILES
These have a .exe extension and, by double-clicking them, they extract themselves to a hard disk.

SERVER
A computer that has data or routing services accessible by other computers.

SHAREWARE
Software that is copyrighted, but may be downloaded and used freely for a limited time after which a voluntary payment is requested.

SYNCHRONIZED DOWNLOADS
Enables you to specify that a particular website is saved to your cache and updated regularly.

TELCO
A telephone company

VIRUS
A program that infects files and may replicate itself and cause damage.

WAV FILE
A digitized sound file format for Microsoft Windows with .WAV as its file extension.

INDEX

ACKNOWLEDGMENTS

PUBLISHER'S ACKNOWLEDGMENTS
Dorling Kindersley would like to thank the following:
Paul Mattock of APM, Brighton, for commissioned photography.
3com.com, animfactory.com, avp.ch, completelyfreesoftware.com, hitsession.com,
music4free.com, neverforeget.com, pcgameworld.com, sailor.gutenberg.org, tech-
sol.net, virtualsheetmusic.com, windrivers.com, winzip.com (Copyright 1991-2000,
WinZip Computing, Inc.), WinZip website screen images reproduced with permission
of WinZip Computing, Inc.

Every effort has been made to trace the copyright holders.
The publisher apologizes for any unintentional omissions and would be pleased,
in such cases, to place an acknowledgment in future editions of this book.